TECHNOLOGY CONSULTANCY CENTRE

TRY THE RABBIT

A HANDBOOK ON RABBIT RAISING

FOR BEGINNERS

BY

S.O.ADJARE

RESEARCH FELLOW

UNIVERSITY OF SCIENCE AND TECHNOLOGY
KUMASI, GHANA

Practical
ACTION
PUBLISHING

Practical Action Publishing Ltd
27a Albert Street, Rugby, CV21 2SG, Warwickshire, UK
www.practicalactionpublishing.org

© Intermediate Technology Publications 1984

First published 1984
Digitised 2013
Printed on Demand

ISBN 10: 0 94668 861 3
ISBN 13: 9780946688616

ISBN Library Ebook: 9781780443690
Book DOI: http://dx.doi.org/10.3362/9781780443690

A catalogue record for this book is available from the British Library.

Since 1974, Practical Action Publishing has published and
disseminated books and information in support of international
development work throughout the world. Practical Action
Publishing is a trading name of Practical Action Publishing Ltd
(Company Reg. No. 1159018), the wholly owned publishing
company of Practical Action. Practical Action Publishing trades
only in support of its parent charity objectives and any profits are
covenanted back to Practical Action
(Charity Reg. No. 247257, Group VAT Registration No. 880 9924
76).

PREFACE

We in Ghana have just lived through a bad period in the history of our great country. The hunger of May and June 1983 will forever be recorded in the history books; the deaths that accompanied it; the migration into foreign countries and how the Ghanaians suffered in some of these lands - all cannot be recorded here.

The economy is down on its knees. Factories have closed down for lack of spare parts and raw materials. The general public cried out for basic essential commodities and the distribution system has broken down giving rise to long queues in the urban centres. High-ranking government officers have abandoned their air-conditioned offices and gone back to the land. However, the agricultural sector was the hardest hit, even though it drew many prodigal sons back home. Poultry farmers sold their breeding stocks for lack of feed. Hatcheries were undersupplied. Meat production in general came to a stand-still.

Now, Ghanaians who have survived this trying time are starting life afresh. New businessmen no longer talk about sophisticated machines, big factory buildings and imported raw materials. The rationale behind Appropriate Technology and small-scale or cottage industry is being thoughtfully considered and put into use by many. The Technology Consultancy Centre has been more often approached and asked to provide a guide. The Centre has done much to promote projects like bee-keeping and fish farming which offer profitable opportunities for small businessmen and hobbyists alike.

Apart from bee-keeping there are other "green pastures" where a hardworking individual may harvest success. One of these ripe opportunities lies in rabbitry, a project which can provide cheap, delicious, nutritious and abundant meat for the family.

Rabbit-raising has been preached in Accra and several parts of the country by officers of the National Rabbit Project and other officers from the Ministry of Agriculture. However, we are yet to see a commercial rabbit farm in Ghana. It is, therefore, the duty of this small booklet to encourage the reader to try one of the simplest of enterprises. It does not require a heavy capital investment indeed, in its early stages, it can be entrusted into the care of a school child. At the same time it has the potential to grow into a commercial venture in the longer term.

The writer of this booklet is convinced of this by the performance of his own small rabbitry. As a busy Research Fellow in the University of Science and Technology, he has little time left over to demonstrate how viable this industry can be. But the little time he has managed to spend in his back-yard has, in fact, supported his claim for high productivity and profit. The proof is there for all to see - one female rabbit having given birth to 34 rabbits in one year!

"Try The Rabbit" has grown from a thirteen-page leaflet, known as "Rabbit for the Family". This popular work, which was also written by the author, has been distributed by the TCC for over three years. "Try The Rabbit", then, is the result of the author's continuing desire to assist in popularizing rabbit-raising by sharing his extensive experience with others so interested.

S.O.A.

* * * * * * * *

As one of Mr. Adjare's bee-keeping assistants, and now a novice rabbit producer as well, I would like to add a few words to this preface. Mr. Adjare does not claim to be a "book expert" on rabbits, although he has studied more than a few on the subject. His authority and knowledge comes primarily from the day-to-day experience of 25 years of rabbit-raising. Considering this qualification, then, the reader can count on finding within this work the kind of realistic advice needed to set up and manage a rabbitry successfully. In these difficult times, especially, such practical tips help considerably to ease the "birth pains" the new husbandry man may feel in establishing his farm.

Mr. Adjare's rabbit farm shows what enthusiasm, motivation and proper management can produce. His backyard operation has grown into a thriving enterprise. This is not to say he has not faced any problems; everyone in Ghana knows that troubles breed faster than rabbits. However, no matter the situation, his seriousness has not weakened. Such perseverance is a good example for all who endeavour to succeed in today's Ghana. I am privileged to have learned this lesson, and much more, from him.

Marlene Moshage,
US Peace Corps Volunteer,
T.C.C.

ACKNOWLEDGEMENTS

It all started in 1959 when I was a young boy at New Banko (Brosankoro, Nkwanta, four miles to Tepa). I called on my master, Reverend Samuel E. Kwaa, who was then the Pastor-in-Charge of the Bechem Presbyterian Church, to give me a pair of his rabbits for a trial. (I stayed with Rev. Kwaa for four months between September and December 1956). Rev. Kwaa gave me two young does and a buck instead. By the end of that year, I counted more rabbits than the generous priest had in his hutches. He was very pleased with this achievement. Consequently, therefore, my heart-felt thanks go to Rev. Kwaa who gave me his animals free of charge to enable me to make my start. Wherever he may be, he must accept my thanks for his support.

My thanks also go to Mr.C.A. Kwashie and Dr.L.E. Newton of the Department of Biological Sciences and Dr.E.O. Asare of Renewable Natural Resources, University of Science and Technology, Kumasi, who helped me with the scientific names of the rabbit greens. Mr. Eric Bosomtwe, Miss Grace Anderson, Miss Angela Panford and Miss Esther Akom, all typists at the T.C.C., helped in typing the text of this work.

There are numerous young Ghanaian men and women whose beautiful works have been shelved or failed to reach completion because they lacked the encouragement of their bosses. I am favourably placed in the hands of D.J.W.Powell, Director of T.C.C. He made all efforts to have this booklet printed.

I should also like to thank Mrs. Marlene Moshage, a US Peace Corps Volunteer, who has devoted her time, both day and night, to work tirelessly with me. English is my second language and, therefore, I could not have written this manual if Marlene had not helped. Both she and her husband, Ralph Moshage, have demonstrated a keen enthusiasm to work for the Centre and for Ghana. Other volunteers whose names should be mentioned are Mr.Josh Dohan (PCV) and Mr. Robert Moss (a British VSO) for their material support and encouragement. Finally, Master Kwame Afoakwa and Daniel Atakora, who care for my rabbits when I am away, and all those who, in other ways, assisted this work, have my sincere thanks.

S.O.Adjare

DEDICATION

Dedicated to my mother, Susanna Afua
Afrakoma of Amuana Praso, who once told
me in her usual soft tone:

"Yaw, try to record your experience in
rabbitry for the benefit of your people."

CONTENTS

(v)

THE AUTHOR

Stephen Adjare was born at Dunkwa, Ghana, in 1945. He followed a Teachers' Training course at St. Andrews Teachers' Training College, Mampong Ashanti, and later taught at Mampong Ashanti Presbyterian Middle School. In 1967 he was appointed a tutor at the Amaniampong Secondary School where he taught Mathematics, Music and Art. His B.A. in Art was obtained from the University of Science and Technology, Kumasi, between October 1971 and June 1975 and a Post Graduate course in Art Education was completed a year later.

In September 1976, Stephen Adjare started his National Service programme with the Technology Consultancy Centre, where he was in charge of Rural Textiles Promotion. A year later he became a senior member of the University staff combining textiles with beekeeping. A self-taught beekeeper he now finds apiculture promotion his main official duty and enjoyment.

LIST OF ILLUSTRATIONS

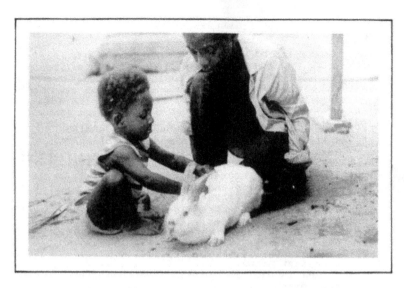

Figure 1. Emmanuel Kofi Adjare and Uncle Dan admire a
Californian crossbreed - note the black nose and ears.

Figure 2. Black Californian crossbreed - weight 5.1 kg.
From the Adjare Brothers Rabbitry.

1. BREEDING RABBITS

The small-scale nature of a rabbitry is a big advantage because it requires minimal capital investment. This means that young men and women can easily afford to begin a project with very little risk involved. It can easily be started as a back-yard garden enterprise. Little space is required and there will be no need to buy a large tract of land.

Rabbits are fast breeders and can produce large quantities of rich meat for home consumption. They reproduce faster than the pig, goat or sheep. One DOE can produce more than 15 times her own weight in offspring within one year if she is properly cared for. Indeed, female rabbits naturally deliver a LITTER every 31 days. However, a doe should be controlled to litter four or five times a year. It can bear between four and twelve BUNNIES in a litter.

Rabbits grow very fast because they are good converters of waste foods into meat. A little rabbit born today weighs around 57 grammes (2oz); in six days it doubles its weight. In one month it will increase its size eight times or more. By the end of the second month, a Californian or New Zealand White will, if well maintained, weigh more than 2 kilograms (4lbs 4 ozs). A bunny takes five months to reach maturity but can be slaughtered at the end of the 3rd month - by which time a Californian may weigh about 3 kilograms (6lbs 6ozs). It is common to slaughter a rabbit as young as two months old in Europe and elsewhere but this is rarely done in Ghana or other surrounding countries.

BREEDS:

In Europe, rabbits are raised for both meat and pelt production. Because white pelts are preferred, the standard commercial breeds are the white-furred varieties. Here in Ghana, there is no discrimination against rabbits with coloured pelts or meat. The husbandry man is primarily concerned with producing the highest grade of meat. Care must be taken to select prolific breeders and those strains which are efficient converters of food with a high ratio of meat to bone.

The local African rabbits are usually the easiest to keep. Although they are smaller than the imported breeds, they suffer less from diseases and so are easier to manage. Another important advantage the Africans have over the EXOTIC breeds is due to the larger number of teats found on the local does. With ten teats, the African can nurse more bunnies than the average exotic rabbit. To take advantage of this capability, select a good local doe to be mated with an exotic BUCK. The offspring will not only be stronger, healthier and meatier but will possess ten teats. This means that when the cross-bred doe produces more than eight bunnies, it can nurse as many as ten. There will be little or no need to reduce the litter size to enable the doe to care for them.

Thanks to the programme at the National Rabbit Project at Kwabenya, there are several varieties of crossbred rabbits available. Some of these are the HYBRID offspring of New Zealand White, American Albino and the Checkered Giant. Around the University of Science and Technology campus in Kumasi, the Californian crossbreed is common. The adult weights between 4.5 to 5.3 kilograms (about 9 - 11 lbs).

RABBITS BY NATURE

Rabbits are RODENTS. They are relatively quiet and rest during the day. At night they wander about eating both green and dry leaves. Like the grasscutter, their dinner time is between 4 and 5 a.m. It is during this time that they enjoy eating green leaves in larger quantities.

Before the rabbit was domesticated, the bush was its home where it roamed about like the grasscutter. Its enemies are the dog, wild cat and the jackal. In the bush[1] the doe about to litter her young ones burrows a hole to make a safe place for her young. She collects dry grasses and soft material like kapok and lastly pulls off some of her own fur from her breast around her teats and mane to dress a bed before she delivers her young ones. After safe delivery, the doe leaves the bunnies and sets off to the entrance of the burrow, where she begins to seal it off. Whilst she is busily working, the buck is impatiently waiting nearby and invites the mother doe for impregnation. The doe, which under the natural circumstance is on heat obliges for the first mating attempt which results in immediate pregnancy. The sealing off will be continued and on finishing it more mating will follow as demanded by the buck.

The young ones are fed on milk once a day. This mostly occurs at early morning or late evening. The bunnies are born blind, naked and deaf. In 11 days their eyes will open and they begin to grow fur. After 14 days

---

1. Wild rabbits do not live in holes as generally believed. They keep their young ones in such burrows and when taking shelter from attack they can quickly go into a hole they have prepared.

TABLE 1

SOME VALUABLE BREEDS FOR MEAT PRODUCTION

BREED	COUNTRY OF ORIGIN	WEIGHT	COLOUR	REMARKS
BEVEREN	Belgium	3.5-4.5kg	White variety	Abundance of meat on back and hind quarters
CALIFORNIAN	U.S.A.	4.5-5.3Kg	White body black on nose, ears tail and feet.	Very prolific Litters up to 12 bunnies but can care for eight.
CHINCHILLA	Gt.Britain	5.5Kg	Blue-grey vary	Quick maturing. Good meat to bone ratio
DUTCH	Europe	2.7Kg	Black & white	Good mothering qualities
FLEMISH GIANT	Belgium	5.5-7Kg	Grey	Could be good for cross-breeding
GIANT BLANC	France	5.5-6.5Kg		Can be crossed with New Zealand White
NEW ZEALAND WHITE	U.S.A.	Buck: 4.5-5.3Kg Doe: 5-6Kg	White	Has been extensively used in Europe
NEW ZEALAND RED	U.S.A.	3-4Kg	Bright Reddish	Good meat to bone ratio

Figure 3. Flemish Giant crossbreed - weight 5.1 kg.
From the Adjare Brothers Rabbitry.

they venture out of the burrow and enjoy fresh air and play. At 16-21 days they have started to eat grass. At 23 days their mother begins to wean them if she is reimpregnated. On the 31st day the mother KINDLES again.

Under such natural conditions the doe has no time to rest. She has young ones in the womb to feed. She has bunnies to care for and she has her own self to maintain. She therefore has to eat voraciously in order to keep her health.

* * * * * *

DOE	-	a female rabbit
BUCK	-	a male rabbit
LITTER	-	bring forth young ones
EXOTIC	-	not native, imported from foreign lands or countries
BUNNIES	-	young baby rabbits
HYBRID	-	the offspring of two different varieties
RODENTS	-	animals that gnaw things with their front teeth e.g. rat, squirrel.

2.RABBIT REARING

As a rabbit-rearer, the important traits to consider are the rabbit's need for accommodation, its feeding requirements, and its reproductive tendencies. This knowledge of the animal's natural characteristics will be used as a guide for caring for them. For instance, the rabbit is nearly defenceless and has many potential predators. It is the responsibility, then, of the producer to provide safe and sturdy shelters to protect his animals. As the rabbits obviously cannot be allowed to forage for themselves, the owner must also undertake to keep them well supplied with a balanced ration of greens and grains. Lastly, although rabbits are instinctively eager and prolific breeders, their reproductive rate must be controlled. Careful management in the above manner will ensure a steady production of healthy and vigorous bunnies.

HOUSING

Rabbits can never be kept successfully under free-range practice as can be done with domestic animals like goats, sheep and fowls. They can easily be stolen and enemies, like dogs and cats, are always around to eat or molest them. It is necessary then, to provide rabbits with a sturdy, permanent shelter. Outdoor hutches with rcompartments make convenient accommodation. For the commercial producer, a large wooden or concrete building to house a series of wire cages should not be ruled out. A single hutch can be divided into two, three or four compartments so that it can be easily transported if the need arises. Hutches must be well ventilated and can be constructed from cheap, but durable material (like bamboo strips) and wire netting and must be designed to keep away undesired elements like dogs, cats and children. Also they must be vermin proof. A large commercial rabbitry in an urban centre can make good use of available amenities like electricity and piped water. In this case a durable building must be put up with good drainage facilities. Water should be piped to the building and electric light installed. Such rabbit farms should not forget to include shelter for attendants and one or two rooms for storage and other purposes.

(1) CAGES FOR DOES: Each breeding doe should have her own cubicle or compartment in a hutch. The compartment should be: Length 107cm(42in); Breadth 60cm(24in); Depth 65/48cm(2ft/1¼). The hutch must be raised off the ground about 45cm(1½ft). The roof of the outdoor hutch should slope to allow rainwater to trickle downward.

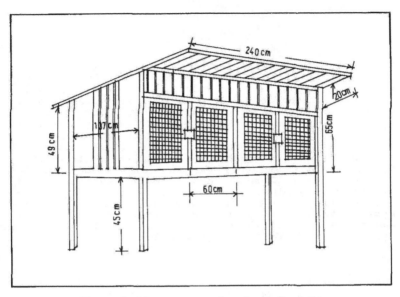

Figure 4. Diagram - a safe and sturdy shelter.

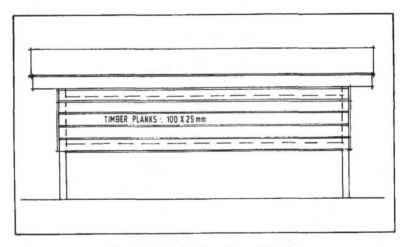

Figure 5. Back elevation of hutch.

6.

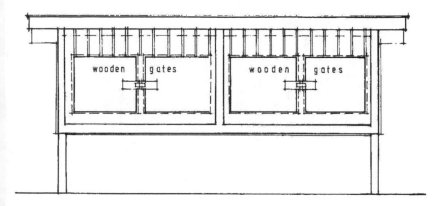

Figure 6. Front elevation - Breeding Does.

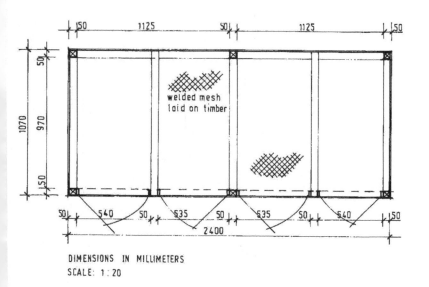

DIMENSIONS IN MILLIMETERS
SCALE: 1:20

Figure 7. Plan - Breeding Does.

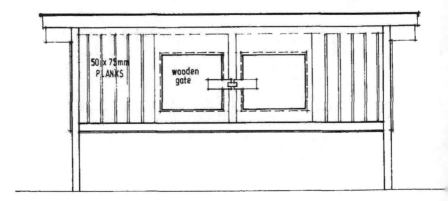

Figure 8. Front Elevation - Weaners.

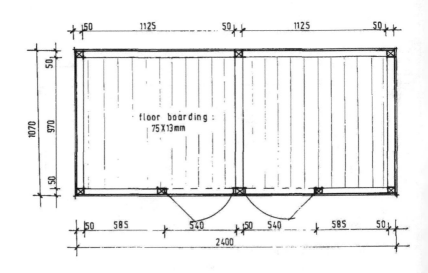

DIMENSIONS IN MILLIMETRES
SCALE: 1 : 20

Figure 9. Plan - Weaners.

8.

This means that the back height must be shortened from 110cm to 94cm(3 ½ft /3ft). The floor should also be wiremesh which will allow the droppings to fall easily to the ground.

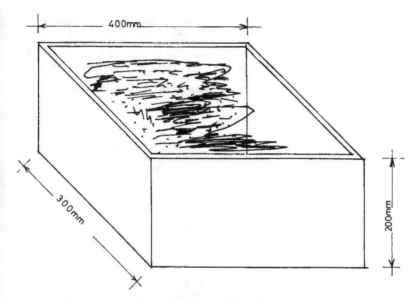

Figure 10. Kindling Box with Bedding Material i.e. dried grass and mother's own fur.

(2) THE KINDLING BOX: Kindling boxes must be ready and installed on the floor of the doe's cubicle at least one week before delivery. This preparation will allow the doe plenty of time to dress her bed before delivery. The box should be easily removable because the bunnies will use it only for the first 14 days. They will then need more space in the cage to move about. A kindling box usually measures 43cm x 35cm x 25cm. Dry rags and leaves must also be provided. The mother will need them to prepare her kindling bed for the bunnies. It is important to note here that stringy material, like weaving yarns or spongy synthetics, should on no account be put into the kindling box. Such material will surely entangle bunnies and can cause great harm.

---

4. "The effect of sweet potato leaves on the fecundity of Rabbits (oryctolagus caniculus)" by E.Boampong, June 1981; Department of Biological Sciences, U.S.T., Kumasi.

(3) COLONY REARING: Several weaners intended for the
market or for other purposes can be sexed and reared
together in one large cage allowing five to share a
floor space of about 90 x 90cm. Remember to allow only
rabbits of the same age to live in such coops to avoid
infighting.

After three months of age, rabbits must be separated;
each rabbit, either doe or buck, occupying its own
compartment. If this is not done, bucks will begin to
castrate each other and there will be fighting and
commotion in the cage which can cause deaths among them.
Does will also begin to ride each other causing false
pregnancies to occur. These does may later refuse to be
mated.

A COMPARTMENT FOR THE BUCK

The buck must be provided with a slightly larger
cubicle, preferably an area of 90 x 90cm. This should
be larger to make room for the doe which will be given
to him to service.

SERVICING OF THE DOE

For efficient production the rabbit breeder should plan
his mating programme so that three or more does are
delivered within a day or a short period of time. This
arrangement will ensure adequate care if some of the
does produce unusually large or small litters. For
instance, sometimes a doe will litter more than she can
nurse. The extra bunnies can then be transferred to
mothers which have delivered fewer than expected. On
the other hand if some of the does produce far less than
expected, all the bunnies of some of them can be
transferred to others so that the mothers whose bunnies
are away are prepared for immediate breeding. In this
case it will take less than one week for the childless
to be on heat again.

Extra bunnies are readily accepted if they are of the
same age, or if only two or three days separate them.
The rabbit breeder has to be able to manage such
situations to his advantage.

(1) HOW MANY DOES SHOULD ONE BUCK SERVICE? One good
mature buck has the stamina to cross ten to twelve times
a day. Indeed, if a doe is left with a buck overnight,
as some authorities suggest, the buck will overtire
himself in repetitive (useless) attempts to mate her.
On no account should the buck be strained in this way.
The ideal way is to allow the buck only one mating
chance per doe. For instance, after the first service,
the doe is removed from the buck's cage. Shortly after

the buck is given another doe to cross. In this manner, one buck can service three - five does on that day without problems. Allow the buck some few days rest i.e. three days is an ideal time. He can then service another set of three or four.

In theory then, controlled mating would allow a buck to mate with any number of does. However, the conscientious rabbit breeder would never repeatedly cross all his does with the same buck for fear of inbreeding$_2$. Inbred rabbits are usually weaker and smaller than normal; any such inferior rabbits should be culled. Depending on the number of does then, it will be necessary to keep two or more bucks for breeding. Or, if the rabbit raiser does not want to maintain his own bucks, he may go to any other rabbit farm and have his does crossed by their bucks. It is important to select only the best animals for breeding stock and to keep accurate account of their servicing and kindling records. Does are impregnated during their heating period only.

(2) THE HEATING PERIOD:
There is a definite heating period for female rabbits. The heating cycle is between 15 and 16 days.

SYMPTOMS: During the heating period, the doe becomes restless and agressive. The vital organ becomes swollen, pinkish red and juicy. A restless doe begins to jump and play about always trying to get into the nest of the next rabbit. If two does are in one cubicle the doe under heat will begin to ride the other and pretend to cross her. If the keeper ignores this behaviour it can result in what is usually called a false pregnancy. False pregnancy is a term given to a doe that prepares her bed by collecting rubbish and pulling her own fur to dress a kindling bed; pretending she is about to litter her young ones. Does seen to be on heat are to be serviced immediately. They readily accept the buck within a few seconds.

WHEN IS THE MAIN HEATING PERIOD?

(a)   Between 15 and 17 weeks from the date of birth. However, this is too early for a young doe to be serviced. Wait until the doe is five or six months old before impregnating it.

(b)   The doe that lost all her bunnies at birth may be on heat a week later. She is due for servicing.

---

2. Inbreeding - breeding from animals closely related.

(c) Some nursing mothers may show signs of heat on the 28th day from the time of delivery. Do not service them. They will be on heat again two weeks later. They can be serviced then.

NOTE: Proper facilities are not available in our country for real commercial rabbitry. In the U.S.A. and European countries, where infrastructural conditions are ideal for commercial meat rabbit production, the rabbit keeper can allow his doe to litter up to seven times annually. This means that bunnies are weaned earlier than 28 days. Due to the availability of good prepared pellets, which contain all the nutrients the young bunny requires, there is little or no infant mortality. It would be possible to do the same here in this country if dry pellets and drugs were available. Since they are not, allow rabbits to litter four times only to ensure the health of both the mother and offspring.

(3) PREPARING DOE FOR SERVICING: As suggested above, it is worthwhile impregnating several does on the same day. To do this needs planning, e.g. how many does and bucks should be involved in the exercise on a single day? For example, newly matured does can be specially fed to enable all of them to be under heat at the same time. Or perhaps another rabbit breeder is prepared to loan his buck for a short time, then it would be especially advantageous to prepare a number of does for the occasion.

METHOD: After 28 days of nursing, the mother does can be removed from their bunnies and given extra rich rations for three to five days. They will be on heat during this time and can be serviced. Serviced does can return to their bunnies if they still have milk.

(4) HOW TO SERVICE A DOE: Remove the restless doe from her cage and place her in the cubicle of the buck. Within a few seconds to about three minutes the buck will service her.

(5) THE SIGN OF A SUCCESSFUL SERVICE: The buck will ride on the doe. The doe will raise her tail and expose her vital organ in readiness for penetration of the male's organ. When penetration occurs, both fall and after one or two seconds, they separate by moving away from each other. Arrest the doe and inspect her to see whether she has successfully been impregnated. You will notice a white jelly-like juice on the outside skin of the vagina and on the immediate fur around it. No more mating is required. Put the doe back into her cubicle.

Figure 11. A Pregnant Rabbit. Note the sagging stomach.

THE PREGNANT DOE

(1) <u>SIGN</u>: After six hours some impregnated does will reject any buck if they are put into the buck's coop. On the next morning the heating characteristics are completely gone. The swollen vagina shrinks and becomes pale. She begins to grow more full and gains weight rapidly. Fourteen days later her teats become pinkish red and her vital organ begins to swell. She develops more fur in her mane. Other symptoms of a pregnant doe are:

> (a) She will try to tip over any container put into her cubicle. For example she will tip over her drinking bowl after tasting some water.
>
> (b) When kept in a large room she will always hide in a dark corner.
>
> (c) She will make some noise any time a buck approaches her.

(2) <u>PALPATATION TECHNIQUE</u>: Another reliable technique

of determining pregnancy is the palpatation [3] method. This involves the feeling of the growing embryos in the horns of the uterus. The experienced operator can determine pregnancy between the 9th and 10th day whilst the inexperienced rabbit keeper can try it between the 12th and 14th day after impregnation. The developing embryos can be felt between the thumb and the fingers sideways under the doe's stomach between the two hind legs in front of the pelvis. This technique must be practiced with care. If improperly done, it may result in the death of either the embryo or doe - or both.

(3) THE KINDLING BED: The doe delivers on the 31st day (sometimes plus or minus one day). Anytime from one week before kindling the doe begins to prepare by collecting dry grass and material suitable for bedding for her litters. Just before delivery she begins to pull her own fur from the mane and around the teats. She will sometimes pull fur from other rabbits if she has the slightest opportunity.

AFTER DELIVERY

The hutch of the mother rabbit must be inspected.
(a) Check whether all bunnies are in the kindling box. If they are scattered about in the cage, collect them for safe keeping in the kindling box. Supply straw and soft bedding material if the mother did not provide some fur for them.

(b) See if the size of each bunny is normal. If any are abnormally small, remove and destroy them. Note that if such abnormally small bunnies are left they will surely die later. This can occur from one day to sixty days of age by which time the bunny has wasted milk and supplies for no gainful purpose.

(c) Count them. If there are more than the mother can care for, send some to another mother doe who can care for extra bunnies. The foster mother should have delivered at almost the same time (one to three days difference).

FEEDING THE YOUNG

Bunnies are fed by the mother once every 24 hours. On the eleventh day the eyes open. They start to eat green grass as early as the 16th day. But supply only fairly dry or dry grass. They are weaned at the end of the 6th to 8th week.

---

3. Palpatation - feeling the developing embryos with the fingers.

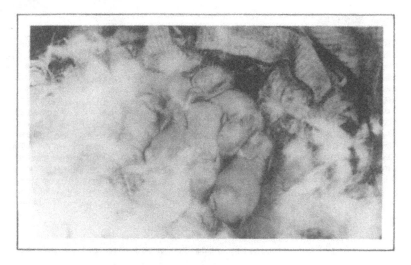

Figure 12. Bunnies in the Kindling Box - ten minutes
after birth.

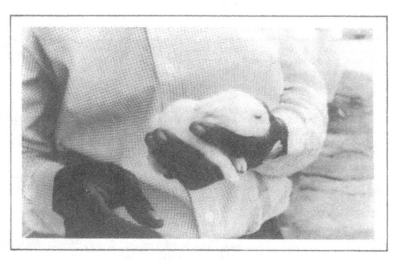

Figure 13. Bunnies - on the 11th day.
Photographed by Mrs. Marlene Moshage.

DEAD BUNNIES

Chilling due to improper care by the mother or the rabbit keeper can cause young rabbits to die. Textile material, like weaving yarns and thin nylon threads can entangle and sometimes cut or deform bunnies. This can easily kill young rabbits. Keep rabbits out of rain entirely. Strong bunnies, like honey bees, can generate heat for themselves when the weather is cold. They do this by forming a cluster. They will scatter about when it is warm. A sick bunny is usually isolated. The mother buries it in the bed . It is important to inspect bunnies every day to make sure that the dead ones are removed instantly. If left uncollected they will decay and cause great harm to their litter mates. A high rate of mortality in most cases can be traced to:

    (a) unhealthy or weak parents
    (b) inbreeding
    (c) mothers being made to breed too early and too
         often
    (d) feeding mothers and young rabbits on
         succulents or on too many immature greens
         (refer to feed).

WEANERS

WEAN at 6 - 8 weeks. This means that the doe is separated from the bunnies. The mothers are fed on extra rations to make them come onto heat for breeding. The weaners can be sold.

SEXING

A client who approaches a rabbit manager for breeding stock will definately ask for a specific number of does or bucks. Usually he will prefer to buy more does than bucks. Under such circumstances, the farmer must be able to select or sex the weaned bunnies. It is necessary to keep each sex in separate hutches. Therefore, the breeder must study the identification of the two sexes. Sexing the grown-ups is easier than the weaners.

(1) SEXING THE ADULTS: The study of the sex organs of the adult rabbits must be done as a first step before learning to identify the weaners' sex organs. The male organ is easy to determine. A good buck has all testicles easily seen plus the penis, which is in the middle near the anus.

Figure 14. Bunnies - on the 28th day.

Figure 15. Well-fed Weaners. They scramble for banku
(food prepared from corn dough).

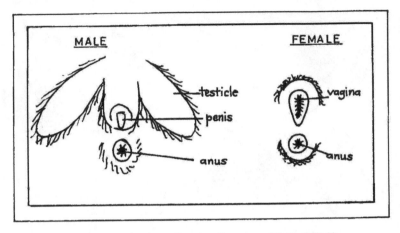

Figure 16. Reproductive Organs - Adult Rabbits.

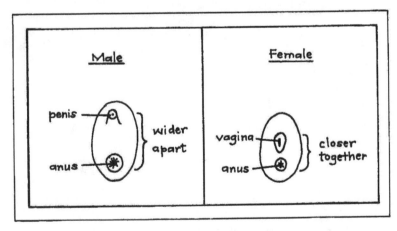

Figure 17. Reproductive Organs - Young Rabbits.

(2) SEXING THE YOUNG: The operator holds the rabbit on its back with its hind legs pointing away from him. The fingers of the right hand must press gently on each side of the sexual organ thus exposing it. The male organ appears as a rounded protrusion and is found further away from the anus, whilst in females it is slit-like or v-shaped and found closer to the anus. Experienced farmers are able to sex young bunnies as early as the first day.

THE EFFECT OF CLIMATIC CHANGES ON RABBIT RAISING

As in all animal production, rabbit breeding has its best season, i.e. the time when rabbits grow well with minimum care. In the dry season when greens are scarce, does litter a large number of bunnies. The novice rabbit keeper should always take advantage of this by breeding more does between October and February in order to make maximum sales of weaners between February and March. It should be noted that March and April are the worst months in the forest region and May and June in the savanna. The new rains promote the growth of new, green leaves but, contrary to the expectations of the animal breeder, these new, immature leaves cause a high rate of infant mortality. This is because the succulent leaves are not fit for consumption and often cause diarrhoea. The death toll in the forest region is the highest because of the high humidity coupled with rapid growth of fungal diseases.

By August most leaves are matured. The improved forage and climate helps most female animals (including human beings) to become pregnant. In November, green grasses begin to wither. Cattle, sheep and goats are content to graze. The females are seen carrying big loads in their stomachs, showing that they are pregnant.

The rabbit breeder must always bear these conditions in mind so that he knows what must be done to get the right type of feed for his animals at any given time.

* * * * *

3. FEEDING RABBITS

Naturally, rabbits feed on fresh and dried green-stuffs and sometimes on roots. Unlike the poultry farmer, the small-scale rabbit keeper should not face any acute food shortages at any time of the year. Even when all grasses are withered, leaves from tall trees and other numerous shrubs are available for food. However, care must be taken as to what can be given to young rabbits, pregnant does and nursing mothers alike. They are particularly sensitive to some plants, such as succulents.

Figure 18. Make use of left-overs profitably. Here these two rabbits enjoy fufu and palm-nut soup.

Indeed, rabbits will consume about 80 per cent of the plants available but they have their favourites, which include groundnut leaves, euphorbia herterophylla (rabbit juice or juice plant), centrosema pubescens and melanthera scandens (wild marigold). They also eat almost all types of grass. But whilst freshly cut, dried greens and food wastes from the house can be fed to the back-yard or small-scale rabbitry, these rations

20.

are not practical for a commercial-scale project as it is not conducive to the quick growth required to maintain large scale meat production. A balanced nutritious diet must be considered as essential for maximum production. But in Ghana, the unavailability of pellets hinders progress on a commercial scale. It is possible for a rabbit keeper to compound his own feeds, which have the required balanced diet, to ensure rapid growth, good milk production (for feeding young ones) and good health.

RATIONS: Green and grasses................60%
            Carbohydrate....................25%
            Protein or fish meal............10%
            Others, including minerals....... 5%

1. Greens: This forms the highest percentage of the required food for rabbits. The marigold and numerous leguminous creeping plants and greens provide essential nutrients for all rabbits both young and old. The Table overleaf lists some useful greens. Available local names are given. An attempt was made to include some common languages spoken in West Africa. Reference was made from "The Useful Plants of West Tropical Africa", by J.M.Dalziel (Plants are arranged in the rabbit's order of preference as seen by the author).

2. The Groundnut and Maize Plant: They provide one of the best greens for the rabbit, but should not be used since there are many other good greens which the rabbit keeper can obtain cheaply. The idea here is that the rabbit keeper must avoid a situation whereby man and animal compete for resources. Groundnuts, for example, provide good edible nuts for man and, therefore, should not be touched until the crop is harvested. The waste leaves can then be used to feed animals.

3. Succulents: Leaves or greens which contain large quantities of water are termed succulents. Bunnies, pregnant does and nursing mothers should not be fed with such plants. After eating them they begin to develop diarrhoea. Young rabbits, especially weaners, will soon die and pregnant does may have miscarriages. Such rabbits must, therefore, be fed on dry leaves. Overfeeding with fresh leaves may result in round or pot-bellies, which retard growth in weaners.

4. Cabbage: The cabbage, brassica oleracea, is a good food for rabbits but it can be dangerous at a certain time. The cabbage is a succulent plant because it contains large quantities of water. Feed the rabbit

TABLE 2

SOME USEFUL GREENS

SCIENTIFIC NAME	COMMON NAME	LOCAL NAME/NAMES
a. EUPHORBIA HETEROPHYLLA	Juice Plant	GHANA: Twi-ahinkogye; adanko milk Eve-notsigbe Nzema-akubaa LIBERIA: Mano-to a gbondo SENEGAL: Wolof-Homguelem S.LEONE: Ti-ebit, yonkara-ebit
b. *CALO-PONIUM MUCUNOIDS		
c. MELANTHERA SCANDENS	Wild Marigold	GHANA: Twi-mfofo NIGERIA: Yoruba-iyawa
d. SYNEDRELL NODIFLORA		GHANA: Twi-ntewadupo; tutu mirika kohwe epo; aguakro NIGERIA: Yoruba-Zanaposa; aluganbi S.LEONE: Balkeyan-karuni
e. DESMODIUM SCOPIURUS		GHANA: Twi-adowobo
f. VERNONIA CINEREA		GHANA: Eve-hosikonu
g. SETARIA SP.		GHANA: Twi-awaha Eve-ebe
h. *CENTROSEMA PUBESCENS	Centrosema	GHANA: Twi-ananse nturumu-nhoma
i. ASPILIA AFRICANA	Wild Marigold	GHANA: Twi-mfofo-nini

j. BIDENS SPINOSA	Bur Marigold or Black Jack	GHANA: Twi-Gyimantwi, akwapim-Ananse mpaane Eve-dzani pipi Krepi-adzrokpii: Krobo-dsethi NIGERIA: Yoruba-abreoloko; akeshin-maso S.LEONE: Mende-tombolo, tombo makei Ti-ebampo LIBERIA: Mano-Zikilli wissi
k. SIDA ACUTA		GHANA: Twi-abrane atu ata Ga-Shwuoblo Krepi-didinglome Eve-afidemii, ademe-ademe NIGERIA: Yoruba-Oshe potu
l. AMARANTUS SPINOSUS		GHANA: Twi-nantwi nkesee, asantewa nkasee nkesee Ga-Sraganmei Eve-matonui Krepi-amma NIGERIA: Ibo-inene ogu, nnuno aku Yoruba-tete elegun S.LEONE: Mende-tahondi Ti-Kanunkuna

TABLE 3

TREES

m. LONCHORPUS CYANESCENS	Indigo plant	GHANA: Twi-dwira Ga-akese Eve-adzudzu NIGERIA: Yoruba-elu S.LEONE: Hausa-talaki
n. FICUS ASPARIFOLIA FICUS EXASPRATA	Sandpaper Leaf	GHANA: Twi-Nyankyerene
o. MANGIFERA INDICA	Mango	Mango

with MATURED (ripe) cabbage only. Cabbage reaches maturity after it has developed a crown. If the crown has not been developed, the leaf can be as dangerous as other succulents and causes diarrhoea in all age groups, i.e. adults and bunnies. It is not necessary to feed the animal on the crown. The crown is usually reserved for human consumption. The part for rabbits is the unwanted, overgrown leaves found beneath the crown. The crown is a good food but most rabbits reject it in favour of the green leaves. After cutting the crown the plant develops several off-shoots through the buds on the stem. Again, these off-shoots must not be fed to rabbits until they reach maturity.

5. **Tridax procumbens**: This succulent plant grows wild and is a cheap plant for rabbit food. Serious problems have not been identified with its use. It is good to dry it for some few hours before feeding it to the animals during the wet season. In the dry season, there is no need to dry it. Feed it to them straight away.

6. **Talinum Trangulare**: The Akans call it bokoboko or efan. A good succulent plant for chickens and consumed by human beings. Although it is rather unpopular with rabbits, it is believed that when a rabbit is constantly fed on it, it may develop a taste for it. But remember to reduce the abundant juice in the plant by spreading it over the coop or on the ground floor in the sun for some few hours. Feed only to the adult rabbits.

7. **Sweet Potato** : It is interesting to note that several rabbit-keepers here enthusiastically supply their animals with sweet potato, ipomoea batatas without noticing the side effects. Such rabbit farms do not usually produce well and the infant mortality rate is often very high. The sweet potato is a succulent plant. Like the cabbage, it can be fed safely to rabbits when the plant matures. But the question is: how does one determine a matured potato leaf? Is it after flowering? Unlike the cabbage it is not easy and, therefore, this book recommends that it should be removed from the rabbit's menu entirely to avoid all the troubles it causes.

8. **Commelina**: There are several varieties of this succulent plant. They are very dangerous to your animals. Any time greens are collected, be sure not to include any species of commelina. It can kill the rabbit, especially the young.

PLANTING GREENS FOR COMMERCIAL RABBITRY

It is tedious work collecting grasses and creeping plants for large-scale rabbit feeding; moreover, such greens are easily soiled during the process of collection and as the rabbit refuses to eat dirty leaves, it is necessary to grow plants which afford easy collection and meet the animal's needs. Thus some leguminous shrubs and trees are found to be excellent for planting. Examples of such plants are desmodium tortousum, gliricidia sepium and several varieties of prosopis.

1. <u>Desmodium Tortousum</u>: This shrub, which is not common in Ghana, is highly recommended. Some can be obtained from around the campus of the University of Science and Technology, Kumasi. The leaves contain some sweet juice. When tested with a refractometer to determine its sugar content, it was found to be between 13 and 14 per cent. The twigs, as well as the leaves, are consumed. Indeed, it has been found to be one of the most delicious greens for the rabbit. All the desmodium species are palatable.

2. <u>Carbohydrate</u>: Energy-giving foods, or carbohydrates, are essential components in a balanced diet. The dried pulp of sugar cane, if ground and mixed with other grains and dried leaves to prepare pellets, is good for animals. The cassava plant also provides a good meal. Collect left-overs, pieces of discarded peels and add salt to taste and dry. Rabbits enjoy them as biscuits. Cook cassava and add salt and give to the rabbits. In the house, any food surplus, such as left-overs, need not be wasted. Bread, especially the crust, banku, kenkey, rice, plantain, cocoyam and banana (either boiled or raw) and palm fruit chaff should all be given to the rabbit rather than wasted. Husk, that is the outer cover of grain (rice, maize and brewers malt) is good food for rabbits. Take advantage of a local brewery by collecting the brewer's spent grain. Dry it and this contains high protein for rabbits. Always add salt to taste before pressing for drying.

3. <u>Grain</u>: Always keep the grain product in well-designed troughs so that the rabbits cannot scatter their droppings into it. Young rabbits are in the habit of soiling their dry food in this manner after which they will reject it, even when they are very hungry. A hungry rabbit will rise and come to meet the farmer when he is approaching the hutch. Some grains should be given with about 0.05 per cent salt added. Salt is an essential part in the diet. Should the keeper notice that the animal is gnawing at wooden material in the cage, then

it lacks salt. After supplying it, it stops gnawing completely but will renew it if the supply is not maintained at the right level.

4. Pellets [5]: Pellets are nutritionally complete food prepared in solid tablets from dried leaves mixed with grains and all the necessary chemicals or minerals suitable for consumption.

FEEDING METHODS
Fresh leaves scattered in the rabbit coop will be turned to bedding material and a spot for fouling. The farmer will think he has enough food in the cubicle for the animal - but it will not eat it. Such greens or dried leaves must be removed. <u>Always hang the greens</u>. Be sure there is enough food in the coop because, like the grasscutter, the rabbit will require food to eat in the night when man is fast asleep. Grains must be kept in troughs or heavy bowls which the animal cannot tip over. Unlike the pig, which consumes dirty foods, the rabbit will eat only clean food, even rejecting greens from the roadside. So make sure to gather food from clean places avoiding greens from toilet and incinerator areas.

<u>WATER</u>: Water is present is every tissue of the body, indeed, it accounts for over 70% of total body weight. Therefore, a reliable supply of clean water is essential. Restricted supply will retard food intake and growth and reduce milk supply. Fresh leaves do contain some water; this source alone will not meet the rabbit's needs. It is therefore a cruel and great offence if the rabbit-keeper ignores this important duty of supplying water. If the rabbit consumes large quantities of dried foods, an abundant supply of water will be required. Imagine eating a local food like yoo ke/gari or a heavy ball of banku without taking in water. "What is good for the goose is good for the gander." Be sure to provide adequate water anytime dried feeds are given.

<u>WATER FOR MOTHER DOE</u>: A doe about to litter must have large quantities of good drinking water after delivery, because she will need it to fill her stomach.

<u>CONTAINER</u>: In the absence of automatic watering devices, the farmer must provide a heavy drinking bowl inside the cage. Any light drinking cup will be tipped over. Special earthenware bowls of about 15cm in diameter with a wide base are good and are not easily tipped over and are easy to clean.

* * * * *

---

5. Pellets - small balls of prepared dry food for animals.

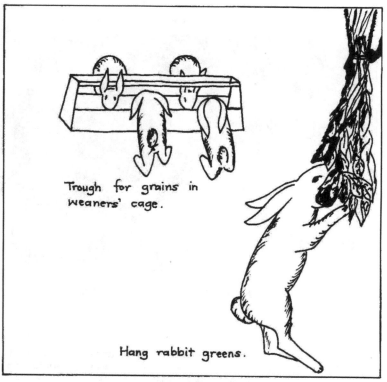

Trough for grains in weaners' cage.

Hang rabbit greens.

Figure 19. Always hang rabbit greens.

Watering jar for rabbits

Figure 20. Watering jar for rabbits.

4. SELECTION OF BREEDING STOCK

Figure 21. A Good Buck - note the round head.

Foundation stock must be selected from among the best to ensure that only desirable traits are passed on. Rabbits to look for are prolific breeders, that have a good growth rate, are good converters of food and have a high meat to bone ratio. The lean little unhealthy ones, the old and the sterile, the castrated and the deformed must be ignored. They are meant for meat and not for breeding purposes.

SELECTION OF A DOE: A doe should have reached adulthood (five months and above). She should be strong and able to defend her bunnies from attack. She should have at least eight teats, all visible and normal. A doe which scatters her young ones around the floor should be culled for meat. A doe can deliver any number up to twelve in one litter but must be allowed to care for only as many bunnies as she has teats.

SELECTION OF A BUCK: From what has been said so far, the buck can mate with a large number of does. He has a great influence over the quality of the breeding operation. He is a very extensive progenitor and, therefore, care must be taken to select only the best to charge with this very important assignment. The buck chosen must be of outstanding quality with the right features and strength. It should be well-built with a round head, sound feet, a broad and meaty body and with a good undercoat of fur. It should have short claws. Look for the testicles. They must be visible and well developed. There should not be bite marks. If young bucks are left in one cubicle they usually fight and try to castrate each other. The buck must show no sign of discharge from the nostrils or any other symptoms of disease. It must be well fed to ensure virility. It will loose weight if made to mate constantly; so mating should be controlled.

AGE OF STOCK AT PURCHASE: Young rabbits are weaned between six and eight weeks. These rabbits are good to be purchased for breeding. Any sound rabbit above this age is also good. On some farms, pregnant does are sold. It is important to know when the rabbit was crossed so that the delivery period can be worked out.

RECORD KEEPING: As in all businessess, record keeping is important. Every doe must have its breeding history well recorded so as to know when it will be due for heating or for breeding etc.

* * * * *

5. KILLING THE RABBIT

1. <u>STARVE IT</u>: Before killing the rabbit, it must be starved for about eight hours. This is done to reduce most of the intestinal matter present in the stomach. Water must be provided throughout the period to prevent dehydration and subsequent weight loss.

2. <u>DISLOCATION OF THE NECK</u>: Dislocation of the neck is the most popular way of killing animals among the Ghanaian community. Hitting the head with a stick is not good.

The blood must drain out from the body completely. The best method is to use a sharp knife to cut off the head from the neck. The hind legs should be held firmly in one hand. The other hand should hold the animals head directly behind the ears. Pulling sharply on the head with a downward and backward twist of the hand will finish the operation. A gap will be left between the head and the neck. Severing the head with a knife ensures correct bleeding and a whiter carcass.

3. <u>SKINNING</u>: It is important to skin the carcass before the body cools down. This makes the operation easier. After skinning, individual pelts must be hung up and never thrown on a heap with other pelts. Otherwise the skins will sweat and stain each other.

Skins can be dried. They must be piled one on top of the other (flat). Do not fold them.

*   *   *   *   *

6. RABBIT DISEASES

Rabbits that are properly cared for, i.e. well fed and watered and kept clean and dry will no doubt avoid most diseases. Curing rabbit diseases is very difficult if a veterinary officer is not around. For example, it is difficult to persuade or force a rabbit to take any drugs. It is advisable, therefore, to keep the cages very clean by sweeping away droppings or manure. Remove all wet food and grasses that have been in the hutches for more than 24 hours. Renew water every 24 or 12 hours if possible. Feeding troughs and water bowls must be cleaned daily. Water dishes must be washed daily with soap. It is advisable to wash the hutch weekly with Izal or other strong disinfectant. Avoid any insecticides as such preparations may be dangerous if taken in by the animals. The only insecticides well known to be harmless to animals are Opigal 50 and Asuntol 50. Diseases reduce the weight of the animals resulting in loss of meat and loss of animals. Try to maintain strict standards of hygiene.

SIGNS OF SICKNESS: The faeces of the rabbit can sometimes give the clue. A sick rabbit becomes dull and inactive. It sometimes squeezes its face whilst the eyes turn pale. It loses weight and sometimes produces watery discharges from the anus, nose and eyes.

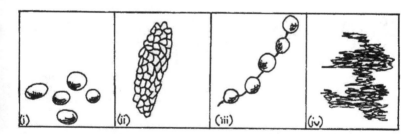

Figure 22. Rabbit Faeces.

(i) Shows the normal faeces of the rabbit which are solid, round and tablet-like. Its fibre content can easily be seen. Its odour cannot be noticed until the farmer brings it close to the nose. However, a sick rabbit's droppings may smell and can sometimes be scented as one approaches the hutch.

(ii) A four to five month-old rabbit is known to discharge small, tablet-like faeces but bounded together in a long cluster. The length varies between two and five centimeters. It is shiny and sticky. It is believed to be a left-over of the edible night discharge which it consumes at night. It is rather difficult to tell the precise meaning of such faeces but some pregnant does, as well as bucks in their puberty stages, discharge this type of faeces - sometimes during the day.

(iii) Shows a discharge of a pregnant doe about one or two weeks from delivery. These are large droppings similar to (i) in size, shape and texture. The difference here is that these are chained together. Does may continue to discharge such droppings until three or four days after delivery.

(iv) This is typical of a sick rabbit. The discharge is watery and sticky. It has no definite shape. Always watch the watery discharge and watch whether worms are present. The worms are round, white and curved with tails. Watery discharge is usually caused by diarrhoea.

1. DIARRHOEA: The commonest disease the rabbit keeper will come across is diarrhoea. This is usually caused by consuming a wrong food such as sweet potatoes and commelina or consuming the larva of certain species of butterfly.

SYMPTOMS: The rabbit becomes dull and begins to discharge watery green droppings. Some forms of diarrhoea can kill a rabbit within 24 hours. Prevent this by feeding rabbits as directed, drying the freshly-cut greens.

2. WRY NECK: A rabbit's neck may become twisted causing it to lose balance. Some authors prescribe total destruction for the cure and to prevent it transferring to another rabbit, but this book is not in agreement with them. We have found that it takes about six weeks for wry neck to be completely cured with no medicine. The disease is not transferable. Mr. Peter Donkor, a Soap Consultant of the T.C.C., had a doe with a very serious wry neck. It took just over two months for the sickness to perish. Please read Mr. Donkor's own remarks:

"My rabbit had a terrible twist of the neck for more than two months. Friends advised me to destroy the animal, but I decided to leave it alone and see what would happen without any treatment. At the end of the second month, the neck started turning to its original position, and two weeks later the animal was completely healed. The disease never transferred to any other rabbit even though it was paired with a young buck in the same cubicle."

3. COCCIDIOSIS: This can cause diarrhoea. It is caused by consuming some tiny parasite creatures crawling round in feeding troughs and watering bowls or on the hutch walls.

SYMPTOMS: The affected rabbits will sit hunched up and extend their hind legs forward. There is a loss of weight and diarrhoea.

PREVENTION: "Cleanliness is next to Godliness", and it is important to clean the hutches well. If the disease persists for a long time, call a veterinary doctor.

4. EAR CANKER: Small mites may burrow under the rabbits skin, especially in the ears.

TREATMENT: Scabs must be removed with warm water and apply palm oil or vaseline.

5. WARBLES: If filth is allowed to build up in and around the hutch, rabbits may develop this trouble. Eggs are laid in the fur of the rabbit, usually on the legs or feet, on the nose and around the eyes and on the fringes of the ear. When they hatch, tiny maggots burrow under the skin to form a small lump under the fur of the rabbit. The rabbit may scratch the spot and this may cause infection.

TREATMENT: A knife may be used to open or remove the lump. Clean it by washing with soapy water. Dilute a small quantity of Opigal 50 powder and apply in the affected areas. Repeat treatment after a week if necessary.

6. COLDS: When the rabbit sneezes and mucus discharges from its nostrils, then it has a cold.

PREVENTION: Isolate it because this may develop into other diseases which can kill other rabbits. It is best to burn a rabbit that dies from an unknown cause. Clean and disinfect the hutch after all deaths from disease.

7. WORMS: Rabbits may have worms. They are white and sometimes coiled. The pawpaw plant is a natural

de-wormer. The root, stem, leaf, fruit and seed, can all expel worms when taken in by the animal.

TREATMENT: Occasionally feed rabbits on dry pawpaw leaves, or mash some few dried seeds mixed with grains and feed the animal with the mixture - probably once in every four weeks. This may help to remove most worms from the animal.

8. A STRANGE AND DANGEROUS DISEASE: A strong rabbit which shows no symptom of any disease or sickness will, all at once run at a terrific speed and bang its head into any object before it. It will continue to do this until at last it dies. A cure cannot be suggested for, even by the time the veterinary officer comes to the farm, the rabbit will probably have died.

* * * * *

7. PESTS

1. <u>DOGS</u>: Dogs are the most important enemies. A dog may kill all rabbits found at a place within a short time if it gets the chance. Always protect the rabbit from a dog by keeping the dog indoors and making sure that the rabbit hutches are strong enough to give the animal the much needed protection.

2. <u>CATS</u>: Unlike dogs, not all cats will molest rabbits. Wild cats are in the habit of doing so. A cat will catch a young rabbit and eat only its nose leaving the rest of the carcass in the coop. Hutches made properly will always keep cats away.

3. <u>MICE AND SHREWS</u>: Some nursing does are unable to drive away dangerous mice which intrude into the hutches and kindling box and eat bunnies. If there are such mice around and they are not destroyed, then be sure that all the young bunnies will be eaten up. Shrews are as dangerous as mice.

<u>PREVENTION</u>:

i) <u>Traps</u>: Traps could be used to destroy these predators. Trap mice and shrews outside the hutch.

ii) <u>Rentokil</u>: This is a good killer for rats and mice. There are other similar poisons. It is very necessary to provide water when such poisons are used. After consuming the poison and drinking water, they die before reaching the rabbits. Always keep such poisons on the ground floor near the hutches.

4. <u>SNAKES</u>: Occassional encroachment of the hutch by dangerous snakes, like the cobra and the puff adder cannot be ruled out. Indeed, as long as there are bunnies in the cubicle of a hutch, a visiting black cobra will be there every three or four days. Whole bunnies may be swallowed or found dead in, or around, the cage.

<u>PREVENTION</u>:

i) Kill them. The only easy way to kill such snakes is to bait them with hard-boiled eggs. The eggs will be swallowed whole but the stomach will not digest them and the snake will die in the bush away from the hutch.

ii) Hutches built with one inch wire mesh will keep such large snakes out of reach of the rabbits.

iii) Grow shallots around, or very close to, the hutches. The scent of shallots or onion will keep all types of snakes away.

5. <u>FLEAS</u>: There are some fleas that infest rabbits which are similar to those found on dogs. They can jump quickly from one spot to another. They suck blood and make the rabbit lose fur.

<u>TREATMENT</u>: Destroy fleas with Opigal 50 or Asuntal 50. About a tablespoonful disolved in one gallon of water can destroy all fleas within a few hours. The rabbit is dipped into the solution or lightly washed with the liquid. There is no need to soak the animal, a little solution on the fur will kill all fleas and lice. There is no need to remove food when applying Opigal or Asuntal. Any quantity taken in by the animal will cause no harm.

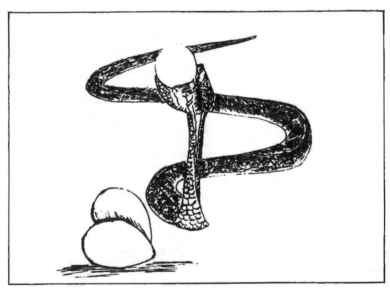

Figure 23. Kill snakes with hard-boiled eggs.

* * * * *

8. HOW TO HANDLE A RABBIT

Rabbits must be kept away from noise. They should not be disturbed too often. Catch the rabbit only when there is the urgent need to do so. Employ both hands - one holding the folds of the shoulders and the other supporting the rump. If it starts to show any sign of aggression or it struggles to get down, lower it slowly into the hutch and attempt another hold. Do not pick it up by the legs or the ears.

Figure 24. How to Handle a Rabbit.

HOW TO CATCH A STRAYED RABBIT: The native variety is a fast runner whose speed exceeds that of a dog. Such a rabbit is very difficult to catch when left loose. However, the exotic breeds are not so troublesome but can cause some degree of embarrassment when they go astray.

Upon spying the escaped rabbit, try to manoeuvre yourself to stand in front of the rabbit. Then crouch down and widely spread the fingers of both hands near the rabbits face. The rabbit will stop and lower its

37.

ears in readiness for arrest. Do not chase it from behind as this will be an unsuccessful pursuit.

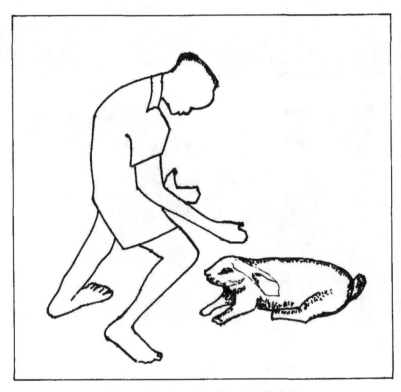

Figure 25. Face the Strayed Rabbit.

* * * * *

9. PERSONAL ADVICE

The author of this booklet has, for the past five years, been going around popularising bee-keeping in towns and villages. During some of his "buzzing-runs" he gives his audience advice on keeping animals as well. He tells a story and at the end of it, asks a particular question. Anybody who answers the question correctly gets a prize of ¢40.00. Below is the story:

"There were large tracts of grass around a village. One of the clever inhabitants of the village, took advantage of the rich pastures which belonged to the people and bought three cows and an ox. After five years his cattle numbered 60. During one Christmas Day, one big, fat animal was slaughtered and sold cheaply at ¢50.00 per kilogram to the villagers. The people rejoiced at this; formed a long queue and purchased some of the carcass."

What were the villagers actually buying?

Please try to tell the answer which, of course, is not "meat".

Grass makes a cow. Therefore the answer is grass. They were buying their share of the grass. Grasses, food wastes and greens scattered around our homes make delicious rabbit meat. The same things produce goats, sheep, turkeys etc. If anybody buys beef, mutton or rabbit, he spends money on purchasing grass (in another form). Money can be saved by taking advantage of the rich pastures around the locality. Take advantage of the grass, otherwise you will have to pay to buy it back from others who do.

This small book provides a practical example for beginners on rabbitry. It makes an attempt to provide most of the information required to start. The author has endeavoured to put down his experience and hoped that all interested rabbit keepers will, in due course, expose some faults, or remissions, so that the next edition will be better than this.

Please send all problems, reports, grievances and corrections to:

Try The Rabbit,
Technology Consultancy Centre,
U.S.T.,
Kumasi,
Ghana.

NOTES